Relate.

Knowing, loving, and forgiving the people in your life

Published by LifeWay Press®
© 2011 LifeWay Press

No part of this work may be reproduced or transmitted in any form or by any means, electronic or mechanical, including photocopying and recording, or by any information storage or retrieval system, except as may be expressly permitted in writing by the publisher. Requests for permission should be addressed in writing to LifeWay Press®, One LifeWay Plaza, Nashville, TN 37234-0175.

ISBN: 978-1-4158-6498-2
Item: 005126271

Dewey Decimal Classification Number: 177
Subject Heading: INTERPERSONAL RELATIONS \ FORGIVENESS \ LOVE

Printed in the United States of America.

Leadership and Adult Publishing
LifeWay Church Resources
One LifeWay Plaza
Nashville, Tennessee 37234-0175

We believe the Bible has God for its author; salvation for its end; and truth, without any mixture of error, for its matter and that all Scripture is totally true and trustworthy. The 2000 statement of *The Baptist Faith and Message* is our doctrinal guideline.

Unless otherwise noted, all Scripture quotations are taken from the Holman Christian Standard Bible®, copyright © 1999, 2000, 2002, 2003, 2009 by Holman Bible Publishers. Used by permission. Holman Christian Standard Bible®, Holman CSB®, and HCSB®are trademarks of Holman Bible Publishers.

Cover design by Heather Wetherington

TABLE OF CONTENTS

ABOUT THE AUTHORS

JULIE

Julie Hunt ("Developing Relationships" and "Strengthening Relationships") is an assistant professor of social work at Belmont University where she teaches a range of courses. She is married to Dave, who leads worship at their church as well as at conferences, camps, and churches across the country. They have three children: Asher, Lainey, and Lucy. She and her family live in Nashville, Tennessee.

Julie loves to read, write, teach, and live in community. She writes a food blog for fun, "Cup-a Cup-a," where she shares stories, tips, recipes, and photographs of her cooking. When she's not packing lunches, talking with students, folding clothes, or baking a batch of muffins, you might find her treasure hunting at thrift stores and flea markets or talking with a friend.

BRENT

When you grow up with an identical twin and huge families in both Appalachia and Germany, you learn a bit about relationships. Brent Hutchinson ("Understanding Relationships" and "Restoring Relationships") grew up in rural Louisa, Kentucky. He's been married to Gwen for 16 years and they have two sons, Adam and Miles.

Brent's training as a marriage and family therapist came from the University of Kentucky. He's currently a doctoral student in leadership studies at Dallas Baptist University, studying leadership, faith, and culture. Brent serves as the community life pastor at Rolling Hills Community Church in Franklin, Tennessee.

Created to Relate
God designed us for relationships.

Think about it. One of the first things God told His newly created human, Adam, was that it wasn't good for him to be alone (Genesis 2:18). So God created Eve. Yes, their relationship gives us the biblical foundation for marriage, but it was also the catalyst for all future relationships. None of our relationships—with parents, siblings, neighbors, friends, roommates, coworkers, extended family, and so on—would exist if God hadn't noticed the need for Adam to have someone to share his life with.

When we make God-honoring, loving, and healthy relationships a part of our day-to-day lives, we're living as God intended. For this reason, it's crucial that we take the time to assess who we are to the people in our lives and how to live in community with others. You've taken the first step by picking up this book. Through the next four sessions, we'll look more closely at the purpose of relationships and how to develop and maintain healthy ones. We'll also address how to restore broken relationships through forgiveness and reconciliation.

Let's face it. We're all imperfect people in relationships with other imperfect people, and this makes our relationships messy and often challenging. The more we can understand God's design for community (with a focus on selflessness, sacrifice, and loving others well at the core), the better friend, spouse, child, coworker, neighbor we'll be and the more glory God will get out of all our relationships.

How to Use This Book

What better way to learn about relationships than in community with others? That's why we've designed *Relate* as a small group Bible study. Geared for a no-prep small group experience, this study is intended to be facilitator led with a strong discussion focus. In each session you'll find:

• "Connect" options that highlight conversation starters and group activities

• Questions to help you and/or your group process the Scriptures and content of each session

• Facilitator tips (*) to help effectively lead the gathering

• A "This Week…" section at the close of each session to allow you to reflect on what was learned and put the session into practice in your personal life.

Understanding Relationships

"Not what a man is in himself as a Christian, his spirituality and piety, constitutes the basis of our community. What determines our brotherhood is what that man is by reason of Christ. Our community with one another consists solely in what Christ has done to the both of us."[1] —Dietrich Bonhoeffer, *Life Together*

Depending on your preferred translation, the word "relationships" is virtually absent in the Bible. In the NIV, "relationship" is used four times. In the NLT it is used 12 times. In the HCSB? Four. In the KJV? Zero. In the RSV? Zero again. If this is the case, then why are relationships such an important discussion in our churches and our culture?

We spend so much time dealing with and responding to our social lives that it's nearly impossible to live and thrive outside of relationship with others. Thankfully, relationships are central to God's Word and to the way He designed us—even though the word itself isn't used all that much.

God's desire for us to live in community with others shouldn't come as a surprise. After all, in Genesis 1, at the very start of Scripture, we read that God created us in His image. Actually, He said, "Let *Us* make man in *Our* image, according to *Our* likeness" (Genesis 1:26, emphasis added). By His very nature, God is communal. The Father, the Son, and the Holy Spirit live in perfect unity together. The Trinity is admittedly hard to wrap our minds around, but it's God's nature, and He wired us with the same relational need. That need is met in our relationship with Him, but relationships with other people are also necessary in order for the need to be fully satisfied.

List the names of some of the people who you know were placed in your life by God for a specific reason?

+

+

+

+

> CONNECT: Divide into pairs or small groups and share pictures of some of the important people in your life. If you don't have any photos, share about a couple of the more important relationships you have and why they're meaningful to you. While you're in your small group, discuss the following two questions:

What types of relationships are most important to you?

When you think about what it means to be vulnerable with and trusting of someone else, what qualities must others have? What do you offer within these vulnerable relationships?

In order for me to be vulnerable with and trusting of someone else, they must . . .

1.

You can't give an honest account of your life story without mentioning the individuals who played significant roles along the way. This can also be said of your faith story.

2.

3.

> CONNECT: As we begin our discussion of relationships and how important they are to our personal spiritual growth, share a bit of your story with others.

4.

5.

CREATED FOR COMMUNITY

Relationships with other believers are intended to be expressions of our relationship with Christ. In his small group study and sermon series *Five Things God Uses to Grow Your Faith*, pastor Andy Stanley emphasizes that providential relationships are critical to our spiritual growth.[2] God places people in our lives, oftentimes for just a season, so we can learn from each other and influence each other's faith journeys. I'm sure you could name several people who fit this description in your life.

King David addressed the spiritual blessing of community in Psalm 133.

> "How good and pleasant it is when brothers live together in harmony! It is like fine oil on the head, running down on the beard, running down Aaron's beard onto his robes. It is like the dew of Hermon falling on the mountains of Zion. For there the LORD has appointed the blessing—life forevermore" (Psalm 133:1-3).

David meant that Christians living like God intended—in community, connection, sharing, worship—was a very good thing. David's descriptions of a covering of oil or the morning dew may not strike us as "good and pleasant" things, but take my word for it—they were to the Israelites. (See sidebar for more details.)*

OIL & DEW

When Moses anointed Aaron as the first high priest (Leviticus 8:12), the oil marked him as acceptable to serve the people. David described unity as something that covers believers, marking them acceptable to God as His representatives to the world.

Mount Hermon was the highest peak around, so it experienced the most precipitation, something coveted in a dry desert. Unity in our relationships is as refreshing to our souls as the dew was to Mount Hermon.

In her Bible study *Stepping Up: A journey through the Psalms of Ascent*, Beth Moore elaborated on the unity described in Psalm 133: "Every time brothers and sisters in Christ study together, worship together, eat together, or laugh our heads off together, amid all our distinctions, we really do get a small taste of heaven. And Christ gets a small taste of His own medicine . . . How good and pleasant it is!"[3] Unity, mutuality, sharing, and caring are all supposed to mark the life of a follower of Jesus.

RISKY BUSINESS

If you've had even just one friendship in your life, you know that relationships aren't all sunshine and roses. They require work, and they often reveal more about our selfishness and sinful natures than we care to be exposed to. Moore also wrote of Psalm 133: "God often uses other people as the chisel to carve true integrity into our rough personalities. A chisel that never scrapes the stone is useless . . . Learning to endure hardship and inconvenience with people is critical to the process of becoming a whole person."[4]

When we share our lives with others, we risk disappointment, pain, betrayal, and a whole host of other negative responses. Before we turn to a series of Scriptures that reveal how to truly understand our relationships—family, friend, professional, or otherwise—let's discuss for a moment some of the difficulties that come with relationships.

What is the biggest hurdle for you to overcome when trusting someone else in a relationship of any kind? Why?

---

*Facilitator: If you want to spend some time discussing the symbolism of consecrating oil and dewfall in Scripture, read the following passages with your group: For consecrating oil, see Psalm 23:5; 89:20; and 92:10. For dewfall on dry ground, see Genesis 27:28 and Proverbs 19:12.

What are some of the risks associated with pursuing godly relationships?

> Every person has one predominant need when it comes to relationships —either significance or security.

A SCIENTIFIC MATTER

Neuroscience, as it relates to relationships, very generally says that every person, regardless of background, experience, and circumstance, has one predominant need when it comes to relationships—either significance or security. Whether we realize it or not, we seek the answer to one of two questions in all our relationships: *Do I matter to the other person?* (a question of significance), or *Will he or she be there for me?* (a question of security).

While both needs are a part of each of us, one tends to be predominant in every person. All relational needs and questions, including sources of dysfunction, are rooted in these two innate concerns.

Subconsciously, we respond to these questions of significance and security from the temporal lobe of the brain, known as the amygdala. The amygdala houses our emotional responses to survival, fear, anger, and pleasure. Those are powerful emotional responses that have a drastic effect on how we view ourselves and our comfort level in any given situation. No wonder relationships—especially the important ones—mean so much to us.

Whether we realize it or not (and most often, we don't), we gauge every relationship we have on the other person's ability or inability to answer these deepest of questions. If we matter to the other person and feel secure in a relationship, it's a healthy and stable one. If either of those feelings are questioned, the relationship becomes unstable, and that's when we face insecurities.*

Which question drives your emotional response in relationships more often: *Do I matter?* or *Am I secure?*

Think about the relationships you're currently in. Was your need to have either of these questions answered an obvious catalyst for forming any of your relationships?

How have either of these needs hurt relationships you've had?

THE "ONE ANOTHERS"
Love
Encourage
Honor
Be Concerned
Carry Burdens
Accept and Forgive

"ONE ANOTHER" COMMANDS

Regardless of the lack of the word "relationships" in the New Testament, Jesus, the Gospel writers, and the remaining New Testament authors all talk extensively about how to live in relationship with others. Sometimes they get into specifics, but more often they address general directives about how to have relationships that reflect God's love and grace in our lives. Many of these directives come in the form of "one another" commands, and collectively they paint a detailed portrait of what sacrificial and beneficial relationships look like.

Look closely and you'll find nearly 60 of these commands in the New Testament. From them, we learn what to do for, with, or on behalf of

---

* Facilitator: This is a brief explanation of a pattern of behavior that therapists and researchers spend their lifetimes working through. If you have group members who struggle deeply with one of these questions, refer them to a therapist who is qualified to treat them. For a list of Christian counselors in your area, visit *aacc.net*.

the people in our lives. Of these 60 occurrences, we're told to "love one another" 15 times. The next most mentioned instruction is to "encourage one another" (4 times). To help us understand God's purpose for relationships, let's look at a few specific "one anothers" that help us model Christ and provide answers to those questions of security and significance.

1. Honor one another.

Read Romans 12:9-10:

> "Love must be without hypocrisy. Detest evil; cling to what is good. Show family affection to one another with brotherly love. Outdo one another in showing honor."

At the outset of these verses, Paul implies that sincerity, rather than fake or hypocritical motives, is an important aspect of honoring the people in your life. In other words, if we truly care about people, we move beyond polite and surface-level and into sincere, genuine, life-changing relationships.

What types of impediments to sincerity do our daily lives present?

What are some things we could do to ensure sincerity in the way we honor and deal with others?

Read also Romans 12:21:

> "Do not be conquered by evil, but conquer evil with good."

What does this verse tell us about ridding our lives of evil and doing what is good?

_____

Why is that necessary if we want to live honorably with one another?

2. Be concerned about one another.

Read Hebrews 10:24-25:

> "And let us be concerned about one another in order to promote love and good works, not staying away from our worship meetings, as some habitually do, but encouraging each other, and all the more as you see the day drawing near."

Why is "be concerned about one another" an important command?

Do you have relationships in which you've made a difference in the world together? How did that experience bond you to the other person?

What can you learn about relationships when doing good things together and meeting together?

The command to "be concerned about one another" in the context of Hebrews 10 speaks to the importance of being a part of a church body. Fellowship with God was never meant to be an isolated experience—gathering with other believers regularly has been a part of the church's history from the very beginning. We must fellowship with other Christians in the local church. I often hear people say they're Christians, but they're not connected with a local church. Perhaps the church has wronged them in the past; or maybe they just like doing their own thing on a Sunday morning. Regardless of the reason, being a Christian without a church is a lot like being a quarterback without a football team. How much good does that do anybody?

The emphasis in Hebrews 10:24-25 isn't on what the believer gets from the community, but what they can contribute to it. If you involve yourself in a faith community by what you get from it, you miss the point.

Fellowship with God was never meant to be an isolated experience— gathering with other believers has been a part of the church's history from the very beginning.

3. Carry one another's burdens.
Next, read Galatians 6:2:

> "Carry one another's burdens; in this way you will fulfill the law of Christ."

In the popular comic strip "Peanuts," Lucy asks Charlie Brown, "Why are we here on earth?" He replies, "To make others happy." She ponders this for a moment and then asks, "Then why are the others here?"

A natural result of showing concern for the people in your life is the desire to help and care for them. When we approach relationships through the lens of Christ, we understand that we aren't in relationships primarily for ourselves, and we definitely aren't in relationships to take advantage when someone else is down.

How does carrying one another's burdens fulfill the law of Christ?

When people are burdened with mistakes, sin, or falling short in some way, what are some specific ways you love them and help shoulder their burdens?

_____

When we carry one another's burdens, it changes the way we respond to other's mistakes. Why is this important for the other person? Perhaps more importantly, why is this important for you?

4. Accept and forgive one another.

Another command that helps us understand how to function in relationships as God intended is accepting and forgiving one another.* But before we look at that particular command, let's look at it in action. Read the familiar story in John 8:2-12:

> "At dawn [Jesus] went to the temple complex again, and all the people were coming to Him. He sat down and began to teach them.
>
> Then the scribes and the Pharisees brought a woman caught in adultery, making her stand in the center. 'Teacher,' they said to Him, 'this woman was caught in the act of committing adultery. In the law Moses commanded us to stone such women. So what do You say?' They asked this to trap Him, in order that they might have evidence to accuse Him.
>
> Jesus stooped down and started writing on the ground with His finger. When they persisted in questioning Him, He stood up and said to them, 'The one without sin among you should be the first to throw a stone at her.'
>
> Then He stooped down again and continued writing on the ground. When they heard this, they left one by one, starting with the older men. Only He was left, with the woman in the center. When Jesus stood up, He said to her, 'Woman, where are they? Has no one condemned you?'
>
> 'No one, Lord,' she answered.
>
> 'Neither do I condemn you,' said Jesus. 'Go, and from now on do not sin anymore.'
>
> Then Jesus spoke to them again: 'I am the light of the world. Anyone who follows Me will never walk in the darkness but will have the light of life.'"

*Facilitator: Issues of forgiveness will be dealt with in more depth in session four of our study.

The story of Jesus forgiving the sins of the adulterous woman is a famous story of radical forgiveness, in spite of legalistic pressures.

> CONNECT: Can you think of a specific time when you needed forgiveness, but you were met with legalism instead? Those times can be scarring. Or what about a time when you needed to offer forgiveness to someone, but you offered legalism instead? Discuss this briefly.

Now read Colossians 3:12-14:

> "Therefore, God's chosen ones, holy and loved, put on heartfelt compassion, kindness, humility, gentleness, and patience, accepting one another and forgiving one another if anyone has a complaint against another. Just as the Lord has forgiven you, so you must also forgive. Above all, put on love—the perfect bond of unity."

LEGALISM
Trying to attain or maintain rightness (righteousness) with God by human effort. Working to maintain salvation rather than resting in grace.

According to these verses, what did Paul say our primary motivation for forgiving others should be?

The action of this passage involves "putting on" a variety of attributes. What does it mean to "put on" something?

This is thought to be one of the most critical passages in the New Testament that teaches us how to understand what relationships mean and how to have healthy ones. Paul described a literal "putting off" of our old way of life and our old character traits ("old" as in pre-salvation), and a "putting on" of something new and virtuous. Dirty clothes off, clean ones on. Bad attitude off, good one on. Legalism off, grace on. Selfishness, no more. Selflessness, a way of life.

Therefore, put on . . .
- Compassion
- Kindness
- Humility
- Gentleness
- Patience
- Forgiveness
- and above all, Love.

> CONNECT: Discuss each of the qualities listed in Colossians 3:12-14 and what it means to put each of them on.

Compassion:_____

Kindness: _____

Humility: _____

Gentleness: _____

Patience: _____

Forgiveness: _____

Love: _____

Based on this passage in Colossians, what does spiritual growth look like?

It's interesting to note how spiritual growth and healthy relationships are so intertwined. Why do you think it was important for Paul to link the two?

WE NEED EACH OTHER

When we really understand that relationships are about modeling Jesus' love, humility, and grace in the lives of the people around us, we come face to face with our personal shortcomings and vulnerabilities. An inevitable consequence of genuine bonds with others is seeing our sins reflecting off the people we're closest to. When this happens, we're forced to either put up walls between us and the other person, or humbly admit our sins and work through them.

_____

But don't miss this: Just because relationships are challenging doesn't mean we should avoid them. Read Proverbs 27:17:

"Iron sharpens iron, and one man sharpens another."

That nugget of Scripture hints at one of God's intentions for community. We can't become better friends, better family members, better spouses, or better coworkers without other people. Yes, we can be imperfect, confused, and even a little dysfunctional from time to time, but our weaknesses don't negate God's design of us.

Keep these four things in mind throughout the rest of this study:

1. We're created to need relationships, both with God and others.
2. The more we come to understand ourselves and how we function within each of our relationships, the better we get at it all, especially at recognizing our needs and the needs of others.
3. God desires for you to feel complete in Him and to strive for holiness with others.
4. Relationships take time and effort. They're not about you, and they're not meant to serve you. But no matter how much effort they require, they're worth it.

Throughout the course of the next few sessions, we'll learn more about what it takes to develop new relationships, strengthen existing ones, and even reconcile those that have gone awry. While there's no way we can cover the vast relationship expanse of Scripture or our real-life situations, we'll lay the groundwork for a fresh perspective on being who God wants us to be to the people in our lives. In the space below, make a list of some of the good things about relationships that make them worth the effort.

THIS WEEK REFLECT ON . . .

> MAKING A CHANGE
Spend some time reflecting on what you learned in this session and what was discussed during your group time. You may have a lot of thoughts swirling around in your head—ways you want to improve the quality of your relationships, a vision of the person you'd like to mature into, and/or a risk you need to take. Try to boil your thoughts down into one key word that sums up your feelings. Confess that word to God in prayer and pray it over and over. Ask Him for a clear sense of how that word can develop into character change or action in your relational life.

> GROWING WITH GOD
- Write your one word down on an index card, or at the top of the box provided below.
- Then write down one of the Scripture verses or passages from this session that encourages you to work toward the vision God has given you.
- Place the card in a prominent place and refer to it often over the next seven days.
- Memorize the Scripture passage you've chosen as a way to have it easily accessible anytime you need the reminder or encouragement. You never know how God will use it in your relationships when you need it the most.

> CLOSING QUESTIONS

Review the "one another" commands you studied in this session. Which one comes the most naturally for you? Why?

THE "ONE ANOTHERS"
Love
Encourage
Honor
Be Concerned
Carry Burdens
Accept and Forgive

Similarly, which "one another" command do you find most challenging? Why?

What is one action step you can take this week to focus on improving the way you relate to someone?

Developing
Relationships

"Wishing to be friends is quick work,
but friendship is a slow ripening fruit."[1]
—Aristotle

Now that we've established that God created us to care for one another and live in community, it's time for us to consider the details of our own lives and our current relationships.

We all have multiple relationships that vary on levels of involvement and acquaintance. In this session, we'll focus on how to develop relationships that are healthy and God-honoring from the beginning. As you work through this session, begin to think about where you see the potential for growth in this significant aspect of your life.

> CONNECT: With your group, brainstorm a list of key characteristics of healthy and unhealthy relationships.* See the sidebar for a few examples to get you thinking.

What stands out to you about the lists you came up with?

+ Healthy

- bring out the good in each other
- point each other to Christ
- are interdependent, but committed

+ Unhealthy

- possessive or demanding
- using each other for selfish ambition
- dishonest

Is this list convicting? Affirming?

Which of these attributes (healthy or unhealthy) characterize your closest friendship?

*Facilitator: Record the two lists on a board or tear sheet if it seems helpful and appropriate to your setting.

What hinders you from developing godly/healthy relationships?

WHAT YOU HAVE TO OFFER

Our relationships reflect our inner lives. In order to develop and mature in them, we must be growing and maturing personally.

I remember when I was a junior in college and was trying to heal from a breakup. At the time, I was reading through Oswald Chambers' classic devotional *My Utmost for His Highest*, and I came across the entry below. His words were stunning and convicting. God used them to set me in a new direction spiritually, emotionally, and relationally. Here's what he said:

"January 7th—Friendship is rare on earth. It means identity in thought and heart and spirit. The whole discipline of life is to enable us to enter into this closest relationship with Jesus Christ. We receive His blessings and know His word, but do we know Him?

"Jesus said, 'It is expedient for you that I go away'—in that relationship, so that He might lead them on. It is a joy to Jesus when a disciple takes time to step more intimately with Him. Fruit bearing is always mentioned as the manifestation of an intimate union with Jesus Christ (John 15:1-4).

"When once we get intimate with Jesus we are never lonely, we never need sympathy, we can pour out all the time without being pathetic. The saint who is intimate with Jesus will never leave impressions of himself, but only the impression that Jesus is having unhindered way, because the last abyss of his nature has been satisfied by Jesus. The only impression left by such a life is that of the strong calm sanity that Our Lord gives to those who are intimate with Him."[2]

> "The whole discipline of life is to enable us to enter into this closest relationship with Jesus Christ. We receive His blessings and know His word, but do we know Him?"

> CONNECT: Take some time to reflect on Chambers' words. Underline phrases that stand out to you and consider the correlation Chambers suggests between our intimacy with Jesus, our personal maturity, and our engagement and perspective on relationships with people. Discuss this correlation with your group.

Now grab your Bible and find 1 Corinthians 13. You may be familiar with this passage, but as you read, ask God to give you fresh eyes to see how these verses speak to the relationships in your life. Read the entire chapter (1 Corinthians 13:1-13).*

"If I speak human or angelic languages but do not have love, I am a sounding gong or a clanging cymbal. If I have the gift of prophecy and understand all mysteries and all knowledge, and if I have all faith so that I can move mountains but do not have love, I am nothing. And if I donate all my goods to feed the poor, and if I give my body in order to boast but do not have love, I gain nothing. Love is patient, love is kind. Love does not envy, is not boastful, is not conceited, does not act improperly, is not selfish, is not provoked, and does not keep a record of wrongs. Love finds no joy in unrighteousness but rejoices in the truth. It bears all things, believes all things, hopes all things, endures all things.

"Love never ends. But as for prophecies, they will come to an end; as for languages, they will cease; as for knowledge, it will come to an end. For we know in part, and we prophesy in part. But when the perfect comes, the partial will come to an end. When I was a child, I spoke like a child, I thought like a child, I reasoned like a child. When I became a man, I put aside childish things. For now we see indistinctly, as in a mirror, but then face to face. Now I know in part, but then I will know fully, as I am fully known. Now these three remain: faith, hope, and love. But the greatest of these is love."

What do these verses reveal about our inner lives?

_____

*Facilitator: If time permits, take a look at this passage in a variety of translations.

SESSION TWO RELATE

According to Paul's words in this passage, what factors define a healthy relationship?

Take a few minutes to assess the current state of some of your most important relationships—coworkers, close friends, family, or significant other. Look at the list of healthy and unhealthy relationship characteristics you made at the beginning of the session and compare with 1 Corinthians 13 to help guide your inquiry. Write down some specifics for each of your meaningful relationships.

How healthy are these relationships when placed against the teaching in this passage?

Descriptions of Relationships in 1 Corinthians 13:
love
patient
kind
not envious
not boastful
not conceited
doesn't act improperly
selfless
not provoked
no tally of wrongs
rejoices in truth
bears with
believes in
hopes in
endures with
never ends

What do you consider your biggest personal challenge in developing good relationships?

HOW WE APPROACH RELATIONSHIPS

Because God created each of us with individual and unique personalities, we approach relationships from a variety of perspectives, and this can change on a daily basis. Consider the categories on the next page.

1. Isolated

For some of us, living in isolation is the challenge we face in developing relationships. Sometimes we're isolated by choice, and other times by circumstance. A few reasons for isolation include:

- being introverted or shy
- living alone or moving to a new community
- fearing the commitment that comes with real relationships
- putting up walls around ourselves for protection from being hurt

2. Surface-Level

On the other hand, many of us are very social and "connected" (if you consider texting, Facebooking, and hanging out as connected). However, when we take a step back and assess our relationships, we realize the majority of them are shallow, vain, or self-serving. We socialize with people, but we don't walk with them through their joys and struggles, and we don't share those parts of our lives with others. We're living in the shallow end of relationships, and we prefer to play it safe (though less authentic and purposeful).

3. Conflicted

We may be very connected and have serious, committed relationships but are having difficulty in one or more of them. A few of the most common reasons for conflict in relationships are:

- possessive, envious, or controlling feelings toward the other person
- unspoken or unrealistic expectations for the relationship
- issues with open and honest communication
- looking to people to be what only God can be in our lives

4. OK for Today

This includes the relationships that, for now, are healthy and growing. For these relationships, the goal is to appreciate what we have and to keep in check the risks and dangers that come with the reality that we're sinful people living in a fallen world. Even when things are going well, we must continually pray for our relationships, remembering that the Enemy seeks to devour things that are beautiful and good.

We're complex people, so we won't always fit into these four tidy categories, but they provide us with a picture of the relational tendencies or patterns we all have. In order to be the best friend, spouse, coworker, or family member that you can be, it's important to discern what personality, patterns, and risks are descriptive of you.

> CONNECT: Discuss these four categories with your group and answer the following questions.*

Which one of these categories best describes the direction you tend to lean? How can you tell?

Where is there room for growth in this area of your life?

List some specific patterns and characteristics of your healthy relationships that can be applied to your unhealthy ones.

Discuss a few examples of relationships from TV shows or movies. What are those relationships based upon? What can we learn from them about what healthy relationships look like? Or what they don't look like?

Now take a few minutes to think about examples from your own life, both vulnerable and humorous. How has trying to develop healthy relationships worked for you, and how has it not worked?

OUR MOTIVES MATTER
In developing relationships, it's important to keep in mind that how relationships are formed can truly affect the life of the friendship.

---

*Facilitator: If your group is made up of people who know each other well, this a good chance for them to encourage, challenge, and speak truth into each others' lives. If not, you might ask them to personally reflect on these things throughout the next week.

For example, consider the story of a friend of mine, Eliza. She developed a friendship with a guy, and running was a primary activity they shared. Their friendship turned into a relationship, which eventually turned into a marriage. John was an avid runner, and Eliza ran some as a hobby. As their relationship grew, they spent time together on weekend runs and she made friends with his running club in the community. It was a bonding experience for the two of them, but running was more of a priority for him than for her.

After a while, Eliza became disillusioned with running and decided that she really didn't care for it anymore. However, she didn't want to reveal this to John because he loved running and valued that she was a runner as well. Eventually, though, she stopped running altogether. This shift became a source of strain in their relationship. Running was time-consuming for John, which meant time away from Eliza, and she felt disconnected from a big part of his world. All of a sudden, something foundational to their relationship no longer existed.

What are some potential challenges this couple faced together and as individuals because their relationship was built with running as the core?

While having a sport or activity as a common bond in developing a relationship isn't inherently bad, for John and Eliza it impacted their priorities, feelings toward each other, and honor of each other.

How do you relate to this scenario? Do you have a comparable story from your own life? If so, consider sharing it with your group.

What are some of the motives (both positive and negative) in developing relationships?

From your experience, what importance do you think motives have?

The Bible speaks many times about God knowing our hearts and seeing our motives. Read the following verses of Scripture, keeping motives in mind.

> "A fool's way is right in his own eyes, but whoever listens to counsel is wise" (Proverbs 12:15).

> "All a man's ways seem right to him, but the LORD evaluates the motives" (Proverbs 16:2).

> "And He told them: 'You are the ones who justify yourselves in the sight of others, but God knows your hearts. For what is highly admired by people is revolting in God's sight'" (Luke 16:15).

> "Instead, just as we have been approved by God to be entrusted with the gospel, so we speak, not to please men, but rather God, who examines our hearts. For we never used flattering speech, as you know, or had greedy motives— God is our witness—and we didn't seek glory from people, either from you or from others" (1 Thessalonians 2:4-6).

What do these verses tell us about the motives of our hearts?

Let's return to 1 Corinthians 13, this time focusing on verses 1-3:

> "If I speak human or angelic languages but do not have love, I am a sounding gong or a clanging cymbal. If I have the gift of prophecy and understand all mysteries and all knowledge, and if I have all faith so that I can move mountains but do not have love, I am nothing. And if I donate all my goods to feed the poor, and if I give my body in order to boast but do not have love, I gain nothing."

Look at each of these statements and consider their meaning and application for modern times. (The first one is completed as an example.)

If I speak human or angelic languages = If I am wise, articulate, and gifted

If I understand all mysteries and all knowledge =

_____

If I have a faith that can move mountains =

_____

If I give all I possess to the poor =

_____

If I give my body in order to boast =

_____

WHAT ARE
MY MOTIVES?
Reflect back on
your list of close
relationships that
you evaluated and
think about your
motives in those
relationships. Be
vulnerable before
God, and ask Him to
help you consider
what you're seeking
in them.

. . . but do not have love, I am nothing. I am annoying, I am a clanging cymbal, I am just noise! I gain nothing.

These outcomes—emptiness, loneliness, worthless-ness—are the antitheses of what we invest our time and energy in. We're in constant pursuit of being valued, making "something" of ourselves, being liked, and gaining all that we desire. Yet, just as Paul boldly affirmed, if we have all of these things but lack loving relationships with God and with others, we gain nothing out of life.

What is magnified in your life and your motives when you read these verses again?

_____

OUR MOST IMPORTANT RELATIONSHIP

Scripture also describes another relationship—ours with Jesus. This relationship is essential to the health and growth of all other relationships. As God purifies, focuses, humbles, and empties us, we become people who are capable of loving others well. That love we read about in 1 Corinthians 13 is something He gives us, that we can then offer to others. It's not a love we can conjure up on our own.

In my life, when I'm not pursuing a connection with Christ, I begin to expect people to give me what only God can give. I become possessive and demanding. Even if it isn't blatantly obvious to the world, it's internally stirring in me. I become self-focused. I see people as a commodity or an annoyance, rather than as children of God. I realize that I'm not loving them with purity, yielding and sacrificing to their needs. During these times, God's love doesn't flow through me. However, as I pursue a closer relationship with God, I find myself drawn toward people in love, purity, and a desire to honor them.

> CONNECT: In John 13:34-35, Jesus said:

> "I give you a new command: Love one another. Just as I have loved you, you must also love one another. By this all people will know that you are My disciples, if you have love for one another."

Discuss the implications of Jesus' statement. How does it point to the importance of our relationship with God?

RELATIONSHIPS IN THE BIBLE

In addition to giving us directives on how to be a godly friend and develop relationships, the Bible also gives us many examples of healthy relationships. Here are two examples:

1. Paul and Timothy.
Theirs was a mentoring relationship with a kind of reciprocal dynamic, where both individuals were enriched by being together and sharing life. Paul guided Timothy in the ways of God and the ways of church leadership, something Timothy could put into practice as he led the church of Ephesus. Read more about their relationship in 1 and 2 Timothy and Philippians 2:19-23.

2. David and Jonathan.
These two modeled friendship, deeply rooted in honor, commitment, and a yielding to one another out of love and respect. Jonathan even saved David's life. We can read about their friendship and the ways it was tested in 1 Samuel 18–20.

How does our relationship with God impact our relationships with others? What evidence of this have you seen in your life?

According to these verses, what should be our motivation for developing relationships?

SANCTIFICATION
The moment-by-moment process of being made holy; the process by which one grows in holiness (i.e. is conformed more and more to the likeness of Christ).

Are you familiar with the triangle diagram for relationships? God is at the top, you're at one of the bottom corners, and your friend/family member/spouse is at the other bottom corner. As you and the other person grow in your relationships with God (or ascend up to the top of the triangle) the two lines become closer to one another. This is a visual representation of the reality that as we each move toward God, the closer we become to each other.

Not only do we grow closer to others as we grow closer to God, but relationships are the context for our sanctification. This is made explicitly clear in the New Testament, where time and again we read that we can only live out our faith and become more like Christ *through* relationships with individuals and the church.

We must have deep, invested, sacrificial, and healthy relationships. If not, we can't follow the greatest commandment:

> **"Love the Lord your God with all your heart, with all your soul, and with all your mind" (Matthew 22:37).**

John Piper, in the sermon *What Jesus Demands From the World*, suggests:

> "There is a sense in which the second commandment (to love your neighbor) is the visible goal of the whole Word of God. It's not as though loving God is not here, or that loving God is less important; rather, loving God is made visible and manifest and full in our visibly, practically, sacrificially loving others."[3]

What is your response to this quote? Do you agree or disagree?

What stands out to you as significant? Explain.

> CONNECT: Take some time to brainstorm (in groups of two or three) commands or directives in Scripture about how we are to live daily as believers—look especially in the Gospels (Matthew, Mark, Luke, and John) and Paul's Letters (Galatians, Ephesians, Philippians, Colossians, 1 and 2 Thessalonians, Titus, Philemon, James). See the sidebar for a few examples to help you get started. Then consider:

How might these commands or directives be accomplished through a relational life? Look through several of them and briefly try to flesh out what this would look like.

> ### HOW TO LIVE AS CHRIST FOLLOWERS
> (some examples)
>
> - forgive (Luke 6:35)
> - do not judge (Luke 6:37)
> - honor one another (Romans 12:10)
> - practice hospitality (Romans 12:13)
> - bear with one another (1 Corinthians 13:7)
> - give to those in need (2 Corinthians 9:7-9)
> - pray for each other (James 5:16)

In contrast, how might these commands or directives be accomplished through isolated, self-protective, and surface-level relationships?

Living out the commands of Christ for our lives is challenging outside of vulnerable relationships, isn't it? That's because we weren't designed to do this life on our own. Relationships are a key part of our sanctification, our pursuit of Christlikeness. They're the context for how we're to live out our Christian walk, and they're the "school" for learning how to live like Christ.

> MAKING A CHANGE

First, take a few minutes to review what you read in this session and what was discussed in your group time. Now think about your current relationships and the areas in your life where you have relational voids that need to be sought out, invested in, and developed. Our relationships shape who we are today, and they can impact our future relationships, too.

"Friendship teaches us to care about another's pain, another's joy. Our friends help us to be ourselves, but they also help us to be more than we knew ourselves to be."

Stephanie Paulsell, in *On Our Way*, writes about relationships being the classroom for sanctification. She states, "Friendship teaches us to care about another's pain, another's joy . . . our friends help us to be ourselves, but they also help us to be more than we knew ourselves to be."[4]

Spend a few minutes reflecting on this quote. Do you see evidence of that truth in your life?

> GROWING WITH GOD

As you reflect on what you read in this session and what was discussed in your group, consider what practical steps you can take toward developing healthy relationships in your life. Jot down some notes in a journal, on a piece of paper you can keep with you, or on pages 44-47 of this book.

+ **Consider your internal life**—your maturity, your motives, your priorities. Where do you need to work on growing and yielding to God in order to benefit your relationships?

+ **Think about who is in your path already**—your neighbors, coworkers, people in your church, and so on. Consider how you might pursue getting to know them in an intentional way.

+ **This week, plan a way to practically reach out to someone.** Invite someone you've recently met to have coffee, go to lunch with a friend, take cookies to your neighbor, or offer to help someone in a tangible way. Developing relationships often requires us to take the first step (as intimidating as that can be).

+ **Think about your relationships that could use some strengthening.** Oftentimes shared experiences can be very connecting and deepening. Consider volunteering in the community, serving at church, or working on a project together with some friends.

+ **Find a project that you could ask people to join you in doing.** Consider inviting someone to help you with a project in your home or to join you in exercising.

+ **Commit to pray for your relationships**—for current ones, for struggling ones, and for new ones. Pray through the following this week:

  - Pray that you might know yourself and your relational tendencies better and that God would help you grow in these areas.
  - Pray that you might have the courage and zeal to live out the greatest commandment (Matthew 22:37).
  - Pray that the relationships in your life would be the classroom for your sanctification and that your pursuit of godliness would be lived out in the context of relationships.
  - Pray that you would be a good steward of the relationships in your life, knowing that they're gifts from God.
  - Ask for friendships. Ask for the wisdom and strength to grow healthy, balanced, godly relationships.

Strengthening Relationships

"When we honestly ask ourselves which person in our lives means the most to us, we often find that it is those who, instead of giving advice, solutions, or cures, have chosen rather to share our pain and touch our wounds with a warm and tender hand."[1]

—Henri Nouwen

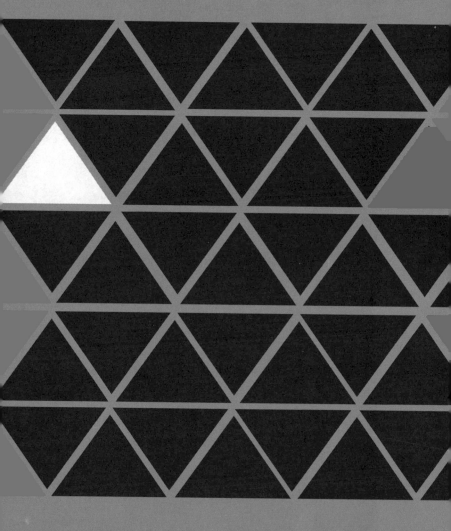

Strengthening relationships is hard work, but the benefits are worth the effort. As we'll learn in this session, our relationships are constantly in flux, meaning that if we care about them, we'll stay committed to seeing them grow. And not much is better for the soul than a strong, growing relationship.

"Anything in life worth having is worth working for."
—Andrew Carnegie

> CONNECT: Begin your group time with an activity that requires work, communication, and trust. Options include working a 25-piece puzzle in teams of two, with one person from the pair blindfolded and the other's hands tied behind his/her back. Or, in small groups, take a set of five images (from magazines or the Internet) and write a story based around the different images.*

Debrief the activity together and discuss the following questions:

Did you find the activity easy or challenging? Why?

What did you observe about the dynamics of your group?

Were you comfortable or uncomfortable working together with the group? What surprised you about your involvement in the activity?

What were the biggest obstacles your group faced? What were the biggest strengths highlighted by the activity?

*Facilitator: When planning this group activity, take into account the personalities of the people in your group, and don't feel limited to either of these options.

The stronger a relationship is and the more you know a person, the easier it is to work together, communicate well, and enjoy each other's company. The easiest way to strengthen a relationship is to have shared experiences over which to bond.

Why are shared experiences such an effective means of strengthening relationships?

In the last session, we listed key characteristics of healthy relationships. What does it take to maintain these traits?

WHAT DOES IT TAKE TO GROW RELATIONSHIPS?
Andrew Carnegie, a businessman, philanthropist, and entrepreneur who led the expansion of the American steel industry in the late 19th century, famously said, "Anything in life worth having is worth working for."[2]

Do you agree with Carnegie's statement? Why or why not?

What are some of the things in life that you consider worth working for?

If you're an athlete, you can attest to the hard work, dedication, focus, and heart it takes to improve and strengthen your sport. If you're a writer, an artist, a computer technician, or even an architect, then you know how important it is to constantly be working and growing. The same is true with relationships.

THINGS WORTH WORKING FOR:

1.

2.

3.

4.

5.

6.

Once we've established good friendships, it's up to us to maintain and grow them. Relationships can't mature or grow if both parties don't put forth effort. But this is easier said than done, especially considering that relationships happen in the midst of work, school, and life responsibilities—not to mention the fact that our culture has ingrained in us the mind-set of wanting immediate results and expecting things to come easily and conveniently. But let's be real: You and I both know that's not how relationships work.

Every relationship—family, coworkers, roommates, dating, friends, neighbors, and spouses—requires work. Different kinds of work and amounts of effort are required for different seasons and different relationships. Unfortunately there's not a formula for this, but it's a fact that in order to grow in godly, invested relationships, effort is a must.

In your experience, what has the "work" of relationships looked like?

While relationships do require investment, intentionality, and humility, the reward is that they should be enjoyable, life-giving, and fun. However, some people feel the benefits aren't always worth the effort. In this case, the relationship flounders in the "surface-level" stage we discussed in the previous session, or it dissolves completely.

What are your thoughts/feelings about the investment that's required of you?

Describe a time when a relationship wasn't worth the effort put forth. What went wrong? What happened to the relationship?

THE NECESSARY EFFORT

Luckily for us, we're not left alone to figure out what it takes to invest in strong relationships. But we do have some responsibility to shoulder. Let's take a look at how our priorities impact our relationships, and then take a look at how Jesus helps.

1. My Priorities

We're one-half of every relationship we're a part of, so naturally our priorities have a direct impact on the quality of our relationships. Think back on the past week in your life. How did you spend your time, energy, money, and thoughts? These are indicators of your priorities. Sometimes our priorities are in line with what we value, other times they're not.

If we say one of our priorities is knowing the Word of God, but we haven't opened a Bible in two weeks, then our actions, or lack thereof, indicate that Scripture isn't the priority we say it is. If we claim that family is something we value greatly, and we're intentional to spend time talking with them and expressing our care for their lives, then we reveal that it's indeed a priority.

> CONNECT: Spend a few minutes discussing what God expects our priorities to be. Think back to what you discussed in the prior sessions to help define where He desires for us to spend our time and energy. Jot down some specifics in the sidebar.*

As we've seen so far in Scripture, relationships are a priority of God's for our lives.

Did "relationships" or "community" make your list of priorities? If so, does your day-to-day life give evidence of that?

+ My Priorities

-
-
-
-
-

+ God's Priorities

-
-
-
-
-

---

*Facilitator: For the visual learners in your group, make a list on a board of the priorities mentioned. If time permits, also make a list of what our culture emphasizes our priorities should be, and compare the two lists.

2. A Growing Relationship with Jesus

According to Scripture, investing in our relationship with Jesus should be of primary importance. We are to glorify Him, yield to Him, and love and serve others in His name. These are priorities that are reinforced throughout the Bible. Strengthening this relationship has a direct effect on the quality of the rest of our relationships.

Read through John 15:1-17. As you read, highlight or underline the action phrases that you notice (for example: "remain in Me").

> "I am the true vine, and My Father is the vineyard keeper. Every branch in Me that does not produce fruit He removes, and He prunes every branch that produces fruit so that it will produce more fruit. You are already clean because of the word I have spoken to you. Remain in Me, and I in you. Just as a branch is unable to produce fruit by itself unless it remains on the vine, so neither can you unless you remain in Me.

> "I am the vine; you are the branches. The one who remains in Me and I in him produces much fruit, because you can do nothing without Me. If anyone does not remain in Me, he is thrown aside like a branch and he withers. They gather them, throw them into the fire, and they are burned. If you remain in Me and My words remain in you, ask whatever you want and it will be done for you. My Father is glorified by this: that you produce much fruit and prove to be My disciples.

> "As the Father has loved Me, I have also loved you. Remain in My love. If you keep My commands you will remain in My love, just as I have kept My Father's commands and remain in His love.

> "I have spoken these things to you so that My joy may be in you and your joy may be complete. This is My command: Love one another as I have loved you. No one has greater love than this, that someone would lay down his life for his friends. You are My friends if you do what I command you.

I do not call you slaves anymore, because a slave doesn't know what his master is doing. I have called you friends, because I have made known to you everything I have heard from My Father. You did not choose Me, but I chose you. I appointed you that you should go out and produce fruit and that your fruit should remain, so that whatever you ask the Father in My name, He will give you. This is what I command you: Love one another."

Now look back at the phrases you marked. What directions are given to us to fulfill?

Which are promises made by Jesus (the vine)?*

My friend Melissa is a floral designer. She has to time her flower pick-up from the wholesaler strategically in order to get the flowers arranged and delivered in a timely manner. Fresh cut flowers only stay fresh and beautiful for a few days. Once the flowers are cut off from their roots in the ground, they begin to droop. With water, the right room temperature, and chemicals to help, their life can be sustained for a little while, but not for long. Apart from the vine, they'll die. Melissa experiences weekly the reality that you must remain on the vine (in relationship with Jesus) in order to live fully and bear lasting fruit (godly character traits).

WHAT DOES IT MEAN TO "ABIDE IN CHRIST"?

The literal translation of *abide* is "to remain or dwell." However, the word can also be translated as "to stand firm or steadfast." Abiding, then, has a definite sense of perseverance in difficulty associated with it.

When have you most vividly experienced the consequences of being separated from the vine? What was that season of life like?

---

* Facilitator: If it seems fitting for your group, divide into several smaller groups and break up the task between them. Have some groups consider what instructions for living are given to us, and have the other group consider what promises Jesus makes about His and the Father's roles.

Similarly, how have you experienced the life-giving nature of a relationship with Jesus?

According to this passage of Scripture, we're incapable of living a life that glorifies God and embraces His grace apart from a growing relationship with Jesus. For most of us, this is something that takes a lifetime to understand. We lack the wisdom, strength, and self-control to show His love to others without His active involvement in our lives.

As Jesus pointed out, we don't produce fruit by being high-achieving, motivated, super-productive makers of fruit, but rather, ironically, by yielding to God, the Vinedresser. When we submit and lean into God—abide in Him—He enables us to bear fruit. Margaret Feinberg, in *Scouting the Divine*, wrote the following when reflecting on a vintner's take on John 15:

> "Just as the vine can't produce quality grapes year-round, neither can we expect to be fruitful all day, every day. Though painful, pruning is one of God's greatest acts of love. Through the vintner I discovered God as the keeper of the vine—One who protects and nurtures us so we can bear the fruit He has set out for us to produce."[3]

It's critical that we understand that *we can't make fruit happen* any more than a branch can; God's mysterious work in us makes it possible for us to reflect Him to the world. However, we do have a responsibility to stay connected to the vine by investing in our relationship with Jesus and desiring to see it grow. When our relationship with Him is one of our priorities, and what we spend our time and energy on accurately reflects that, we put ourselves in a position to be used by Him. And to what end?

"This is what I command you: Love one another" (John 15:17).

According to verse 17, the point of all of this abiding, submitting, and bearing fruit is to love others—to give evidence of God's love and grace in the context of relationships!

What does John 15:17 mean to you?

What are the implications of this verse on your daily life?*

GAUGING YOUR RELATIONAL STRENGTH

In Scripture, "fruit" is used metaphorically as the indication of what's going on inside the tree or vine. If our relationship with God is at an unhealthy place, then bad fruit (negative characteristics and actions) will be evident. On the other hand, if our relationship with God is growing, then God-honoring fruit will be produced. And whatever's going on between us and God has a direct impact on us and others.

In the box below, make a list of some of the current relationships in your life; for each of them, consider:

- Is the relationship strong? If so, what are its strengths?
- What kind of "fruit" is being produced?
- How am I yielding/sacrificing in this relationship?
- Where is there room for growth?

*Facilitator: Spend some time discussing these two questions with your group. Challenge them to think outside of the obvious implications.

In Galatians, Paul provides us with a list of qualities our lives will exhibit when we're growing in our relationship with Jesus. This list, known as the "fruit of the Spirit," isn't exhaustive, but it is a good representation of how a healthy relationship with Jesus impacts how we relate to others. As you read this list, think about how practically, in the context of your relationships, this fruit is evidenced. Read Galatians 5:22-23:

FRUIT OF THE SPIRIT

LOVE

JOY

PEACE

PATIENCE

KINDNESS

GOODNESS

FAITH

GENTLENESS

SELF-CONTROL

"But the fruit of the Spirit is love, joy, peace, patience, kindness, goodness, faith, gentleness, self-control. Against such things there is no law."

> CONNECT: As a group, share specific examples of how your relationships exhibit any of the fruits of the Spirit from Galatians 5. Talk through the following list of questions.

How is this evidenced in the way we value, respect, and serve the people in our lives?

How is this evidenced in the way we communicate with the people in our lives?

How are you communicating with people in a healthy, fruitful way? Where is there room for improvement in this area?

Author and professor David Benner, in his book *Sacred Companions*, describes the quality of communication and dialogue found in spiritual friendships:

"Spiritual friends share with each other at the level of their soul. This does not mean that they talk about only serious, personal or spiritual matters. However, if they never share at this level, the relationship is not worthy of being called a spiritual—or soul—friendship. Sharing at the level of their souls means that their intimacy is not restricted to experiences with the external world . . . Friends who enjoy soul intimacy never settle for gossip or simple information exchange. Instead they use the data of events as springboards for the sharing of feelings, perceptions, values, ideas, and opinions. The conversations of such friends are never merely about what happened in their lives or the world but move from this to how they experience, react to, and understand what happened. Dialogue continually moves from the surface to the depths, from the external to the internal. This is the crucial distinctive of dialogue in spiritual friendships."[4]

> Friends who enjoy soul intimacy never settle for gossip or simple information exchange. Instead they use the data of events as springboards for the sharing of feelings, perceptions, values, ideas and opinions.

Underline or highlight the key attributes of spiritual friendships in Benner's quote. Which of your relationships come to mind when you think about these characteristics?

The type of life sharing Benner describes takes time, vulnerability, intentionality, and investment. Are your friendships marked by this type of dialogue and commitment? Or do you tend to keep people at a "safe" distance?

> CONNECT: Get into smaller groups of three or four to discuss what communication and sharing looks like in your current relationships and where growth is needed. Consider the relationships, past or present, in which you've sensed a rich, honest, and helpful exchange of thoughts and feelings. Discuss why those relationships were successful.

STAY CONNECTED TO GOD

When I'm struggling in my relationships with others, I don't always stop to consider that my connection with God (or lack of connection) could be the cause of the disconnect, and therefore a key to enriching those relationships.

When I'm seeking God for my security, identity, strength, and priorities, a life of godly, humble love flows naturally from that relationship. However, when I'm struggling to do things on my own and live disconnected from Him, I've noticed that I have nothing beneficial to give others. Instead of growing, sacrificial, and loving relationships with others, my expectations are off, and I look to people to be something only God can be. Or at other times, I turn to relationships for my own selfish gain.

Spend a few minutes thinking about how your relationships with others are affected by your relationship with God. What happens to your relationships when you feel close to God, and what happens when you feel distant from Him?

Our natural tendencies when disconnected from God are reflective of the approaches to relationships we looked at in the previous session (isolated, surface-level, conflicted, OK for today).

Which of those categories did you most connect with?

What connection do you see between that approach to relationships and your communion with God?

Short-term mission trips have a way of strengthening our relationship with God like few other things can. This doesn't happen because we're away from home, but because we're a part of an experience that's been prayed for extensively. For months prior to a trip, both people who are going and people who are supporting blanket the trip in prayer. Then during the trip, people back home are praying for the ministry that will happen while the group is gone, and the group spends significant amounts of time each day in prayer, Bible study, and encouragement.

Each day is lived intentionally looking for opportunities to love and serve teammates and the people in the community the group is visiting. The result is a level of compassion, humility, servanthood, tolerance, care, and love for others that far exceeds our normal routines.

If you've ever been on a mission trip, does this description resonate with your experience? How were your relationships with God and others affected by the experience?

When we're connected to God, seeking Him, abiding in Him, and yielding to Him, we overflow with love for others. Relationships become about us showing love, rather than seeking approval; us enjoying the company of others, rather than manipulating circumstances to meet our needs. The challenge we face is living our normal, daily lives that intentionally. But it can happen.

> CONNECT: Discuss the practical aspects of living intentionally committed to your relationship with God.

In the book *A Simple Path*, Mother Teresa and Sister Kateri describe this connection:

> "There is only one love and this is the love of God. Once we love God deeply enough we will love our neighbor to the same extent because, as we grow in our love for God, we grow to respect all that He has created and to recognize and appreciate all the gifts He has given us. Then naturally we want to take care of all of them."[5]

"There is only one love and this is the love of God. Once we love God deeply enough we will love our neighbor to the same extent."
—Mother Teresa

Respond to this perspective. Have you found this to be true in your life?

> MAKING A CHANGE

We all desire for relationships to be fun, easy, reciprocal, and life-giving. The struggle is to find the balance between the work and effort relationships require and the freedom and enjoyment strong ones produce. Spend some time this week reviewing what you learned in this session and working through the following questions. Use the notes pages provided to jot down your thoughts.

1. Growing with God
- What priority am I placing on my relationship with God?
- What is the evidence of this?
- How could I place greater effort into growing in this relationship?
- How might that help me to strengthen my relationships?

2. Growing with Others
- Which relationships in my life are bearing fruit?
- Which relationships are not?
- What is God prompting me to do in response to this?

3. Taking the Next Step
- What tangible actions might I take to strengthen my relationships with coworkers, neighbors, roommates, friends, my significant other, and family members?

Download and listen to the song "By Our Love" sung by Christy Nockels. As you listen to the song, ask God to guide your thoughts as you consider your life and the sobering claim from the song, "They will know us by our love." Spend time praying for God's guidance and wisdom as you begin the process of strengthening your relationships for the health of your life, the good of others, and the glory of God.

> GROWING WITH GOD

"But the fruit of the Spirit is love, joy, peace, patience, kindness, goodness, faith, gentleness, self-control. Against such things there is no law" (Galatians 5:22-23).

With the fruit of the Spirit on the brain this week, take the opportunity to catalog evidences of the "fruit" you see in your relationships and times when you exhibit the opposite of that fruit. See if you can detect any patterns:

When you're stressed, what happens?

Are certain fruits only evidenced around certain people?

In which relationships are you most selfish? Most selfless? And so on.

FRUIT OF THE SPIRIT
LOVE
JOY
PEACE
PATIENCE
KINDNESS
GOODNESS
FAITH
GENTLENESS
SELF-CONTROL

Use this activity as an opportunity to thank God for the times He works through you to reflect Him to the world. Also confess to Him and ask for help in the times your selfish nature takes control.

Restoring Relationships

"The greatest happiness of life is the conviction that we are loved—loved for ourselves, or rather, loved in spite of ourselves."[1]

—Victor Hugo

As we all know, relationships can be very difficult. But more often than not, they're worth whatever amount of effort is required. Whether it's our families, friends, coworkers, or people who have been in and out of our lives over the years, the marks of human influence on us are significant.

We're created for relationship with God; that relationship is expressed in many ways through our relationships with others. But sometimes those relationships go terribly wrong. People have the power to wound and scar us. The more we love someone, the deeper they can hurt us. And we have the same ability to hurt others. When the unity of a relationship is disrupted, we call that disruption "conflict." I don't know anyone who likes that word.

WHAT IS CONFLICT AND HOW DOES IT AFFECT US?
Technically, *conflict* is defined as "a fight, battle, or struggle, especially a prolonged struggle; strife; controversy; quarrel between parties; discord of action, feeling, or effect; antagonism or opposition, as of interests or principles: a conflict of ideas."

Unaddressed conflict affects more than just our spirits. In his book *The Peacemaker*, Ken Sande, a lawyer and full-time Christian mediator, writes, "Conflicts steal time, energy, money, and opportunities for better things. When Christians are fighting, our battles overshadow anything we try to tell the world about Jesus."[2] Failed and broken relationships have a drastic effect on our lives, and the lives of those involved, which makes it all the more important that we understand why and how to seek restoration whenever possible.

Think about all the different relationships in your life. Chances are, at some time or another you've faced conflict in each relationship you're in. And if you've lost friendships along the way, there's a good chance conflict that wasn't handled well led to the end of that relationship. Did you disagree with a professor or coach in college? Ever have a fight with your sibling in the back seat of Mom's car? Treat a coworker rudely because he/she got on your last nerve? Go to bed angry at a spouse over miscommunication? Fill in the blank with your own relationships, but I doubt you'll have to look far to see evidence of discord.

Conflict is an inevitable consequence of doing life with others. And while no one would choose conflict over peace, it's not always a bad thing. Sometimes we have to work through our disagreements and issues with others in order to build a healthy relationship rooted in mutual understanding and integrity. If discord arises from standing up for who you are and what you believe, then it's worth it.

But there are other times when discord in a relationship cuts us down deep in the core of who we are. It has the power to tap into our fears and insecurities and reopen old wounds from our pasts. This is the kind we're all prone to avoid, and it's what makes us resistant to conflict in the first place.

To gauge the presence of conflict in your life today, list the names of anyone you're currently having issues with. Next to the name, record whether you consider the conflict healthy or unhealthy.

Sometimes we have to work through our disagreements and issues with others in order to build a healthy relationship rooted in mutual understanding and integrity.

• Friends:

• Spouse:

• Coworkers:

• Family members:

• Neighbors:

• Classmates:

_____

DEALING WITH CONFLICT

The effect of conflict on you and your relationship is impacted by 1) how much that person means to you, 2) the source of the conflict, and 3) how both of you respond. When we face conflict with a coworker, it can be an annoying and persistent burden until we deal with it. But when a spouse or loved one hurts us, it can be heartbreaking.

Psychologists have concluded that everyone responds to conflict in one of three ways—move away (flight), move against (fight), or move toward (peace).[3] Here's how those reactions break down:

1. Move Away

The flight response is an attempt to avoid conflict by withdrawing from the situation. Some characteristics of this response include blame-shifting, denial, avoidance, ignoring, or postponing conflict.

2. Move Against

The fight response is a defensive, self-protective response where the motivation is to protect yourself by getting what you want. Characteristics include insults, gossip, aggression, and competition.

3. Move Toward

The peaceful response is also the healthy response, where the goal is restoration and harmony. The good of the relationship is more important than self protection. Characteristics include communication, accountability, mediation, accommodation, collaboration, persistence, and compromise.

Think about how you've handled conflict lately. Which of these three responses is your natural reaction to conflict? Have any circumstances led you to react differently? Why?

> CONNECT: Discuss these three responses to conflict with your group. Think about the positive and negative aspects of each reaction.*

---

*Facilitator: Consider charting each person's natural response to conflict to see how your group shapes up.

SESSION FOUR RELATE

Our engagement or disengagement in challenging relationships is a lot like the moral struggle we face each day. When it comes to taking the high road of restoration and peacemaking, our problem isn't usually in *knowing* what's right, but in *choosing to do* what's right.

FAMILY STRIFE

Now that we have a general understanding of conflict and typical responses, let's take a look at a biblical example in Genesis 4, in which Moses recounts the story of Cain and Abel, the sons of Adam and Eve. If you know the story well, you might be thinking, *This is a bit extreme. I've never had a relationship end in murder.* However, you might be surprised how much we can learn from this story. (By the way, murder is the extreme act of the "fight" response to conflict.)

> "The best families and the best friendships are only shadows of what relationships should be and could be but for sin."

Any relationship consists of two sinful people whose natural default is sinfulness. Unfortunately, the more closely you do life with someone, the more clearly you see their sin, and they see yours. Are we prone to murder our biological brothers and sisters like we'll read in Cain and Abel's story? Thankfully, no. But we are susceptible to sin nonetheless, and it infiltrates all of our relationships, making them less than they were designed to be. As one Bible commentator puts it, "The best families and the best friendships are only shadows of what relationships should be and could be but for sin."[4]

Spend a few minutes reading Genesis 4:1-16. Then re-read verses 3-8:

> "In the course of time Cain presented some of the land's produce as an offering to the LORD. And Abel also presented an offering—some of the firstborn of his flock and their fat portions. The LORD had regard for Abel and his offering, but He did not have regard for Cain and his offering. Cain was furious, and he looked despondent.
>
> "Then the LORD said to Cain, 'Why are you furious? And why do you look despondent? If you do what is right, won't you be accepted? But if you do not do what is right, sin is crouching at the door. Its desire is for you, but you must rule over it.'

"Cain said to his brother Abel, 'Let's go out to the field.' And while they were in the field, Cain attacked his brother Abel and killed him."

Highlight or underline the words and phrases that describe Cain's emotions and attitude. What can you conclude about Cain's character from these phrases?

Have you ever thought of sin waiting to ambush you (Genesis 4:7)? What images come to mind when you think about sin in that way?

From what we read in Scripture, the conflict between Cain and Abel began when God rejected Cain's offering, sending Cain into a jealous tailspin that eventually led to murder. While this passage doesn't explicitly state why God favored Abel's sacrifice, Cain's furious response suggests that the offering was rejected because of the motive behind the offering—the sin in his heart. Abel wasn't sinless, but we can assume that the motivation behind his offering was pure and good, which emphasizes that Cain's was not. The apostle John also hints at that same explanation in 1 John 3:11-12:

> "For this is the message you have heard from the beginning: We should love one another, unlike Cain, who was of the evil one and murdered his brother. And why did he murder him? Because his works were evil, and his brother's were righteous."

Cain murdered his brother (Genesis 4:8), and John implied that he did so because he resented Abel's righteousness before God. In the book *Creation Unraveled*, a look at the gospel in Genesis 1–11, coauthor Halim Suh describes what Cain might have been thinking: "Through Cain's eyes, it could've seemed that Abel was a threat to him, because as long as Abel was around, God would never notice Cain. For Cain to be happy and have what he felt he deserved, Abel had to go."[5]

Human nature hasn't changed much since the days of Cain and Abel. When one Christian hates or resents another, it usually stems from a feeling of guilt or insecurity about his or her own life, often his or her sinfulness. (See the sidebar for three steps to identifying sin in your life.)

Think about the relationships in your life in need of restoration. Does this ring true for any of them?

3 Ways to Identify Sin in Your Life

We all get distracted at times, and before we realize it, sin sneakily creeps in. The first step to eliminating sin is recognizing it.

1. Be aware.

Spend time each morning confessing and letting go, so you're ready to face the day with a fresh approach.

2. Be in tune.

You know the Holy Spirit is on your side; all you have to do is listen.

3. Be willing.

In your prayer time, ask God to reveal the areas in your life that need work.

A VERY REAL ENEMY

Think about how God designed the world. Sin didn't fit into that design, but once it entered the picture it launched a vicious cycle. Adam and Eve were banished from Eden, Cain killed Abel, and the pattern continued. While we have a nature that's prone to sin, we must understand how Satan schemes for sin to victimize us. Consider the following verses:

"If you do what is right, won't you be accepted? But if you do not do what is right, sin is crouching at the door. Its desire is for you, but you must rule over it" (Genesis 4:7).

"Put on the full armor of God so that you can stand against the tactics of the Devil" (Ephesians 6:11).

"Therefore, submit to God. But resist the Devil, and he will flee from you. Draw near to God, and He will draw near to you" (James 4:7-8a).

How is Satan described in these verses? How have you seen this to be an accurate description in his schemes against you?

While we often make poor choices when it comes to sin, and we must own them and their consequences, we also must remember that we're fighting a battle against a very real Enemy with very real intentions to draw us away from God. Shifting our focus and energy to our interpersonal relationships is an easy way to distract us.

SIN'S IMPACT ON OUR RELATIONSHIPS

When Cain sinned and gave in to the temptations of Satan, his relationships were drastically affected. Not only was his brother dead, but he was banished from his homeland and all his previous relationships were over. More importantly, however, sin drove a wedge between Cain and God.

In Genesis 4:15, God extended mercy to Cain by protecting him and issuing a warning against anyone who would try to harm him and avenge Abel's death. But how did Cain respond to God's forgiveness and mercy? He walked away from God.*

> **"Then Cain went out from the Lord's presence and lived in the land of Nod, east of Eden" (Genesis 4:16).**

Cain's departure from God's presence was both physical and spiritual. Jonah did the same thing when he tried to avoid God's call on his life (see Jonah 1:3,10). Read what one author wrote about the ramification of Cain's sin on his relationships:

> "In the Bible, a person's blood is directly connected to his soul. Here, in a chilling image, Abel's blood cries out from the ground, which is personified as opening her mouth to swallow Abel's blood. Once he has defiled the earth with his brother's blood, the soil shall no longer yield her strength to Cain. Because of his unbridled rage, the soil he tills becomes

---

*Facilitator: Have people in your group read Genesis 4:16 from various translations of Scripture to reiterate Cain's decision.

barren and Cain the farmer becomes alienated from the source of his sustenance and nurture. When we allow the beast of emotional or physical violence to force its way into our lives, we poison our most intimate relationships, until they too no longer yield [their] strength to us. We banish ourselves from the relationships that nurture us most."[6]

Inevitably, sin has a significant—and always negative—impact on our relationships with others.

How does sin poison our most intimate relationships?

Think about your family. What lasting impact has sin had on the relationships within your family?

Also think about past friendships you've had. Did any of them come to an end because sin drove a wedge between you and your friend?

I grew up with a large, close-knit extended family—that's typical for Appalachian families. It's also typical for these large, caring Appalachian families to know each other's business and to try to keep problems concealed—the family in Appalachia is the primary source of healing, counsel, and nurture. In one of my distant relative's homes, stories of abuse and control on the part of the husband/father were kept secret for years.

As a result, the cycle of violence and dysfunction carried over into every home the children who grew up in that family created. Literally, the sins of the father recreated themselves in one form or another among seven children, their children, and now the third generation removed from that dark house. Abuse, addiction, and apathy are that family's legacy. What's missing? To an outsider looking in, it's obvious: That family needs the peace and love of Jesus to generate healing and break its horrific pattern.

Whether or not your stories of conflict are as extreme as my extended family's, you're equally as dependent on the peace of Jesus to change your bad patterns in relationships.

GOD'S EXAMPLE OF RESTORATION

SETH
The name "Seth" means "He set or appointed" or "replacement." It is a wordplay on the Hebrew verb translated "has given." Eve saw Seth as a gift from God to replace the sons she lost.

If you read the rest of Cain's story (Genesis 4:17-24), you see the impact of Cain's sin on his future generations. The sin in which his descendents found themselves broke their relationships entirely, and both their interactions with each other and with God were defined by self-gratifying behavior.

But, as God would eventually do for all of humanity when Jesus died on the cross, He redeemed the pain Cain's actions left on his family and restored His people back to Himself:

"Adam was intimate with his wife again, and she gave birth to a son and named him Seth, for she said, 'God has given me another child in place of Abel, since Cain killed him.' A son was born to Seth also, and he named him Enosh. At that time people began to call on the name of Yahweh" (Genesis 4:25-26).

God blessed Adam and Eve with another son. When Cain killed Abel, Adam and Eve lost both their sons. Abel died; Cain was banished. The pain they experienced had to be life-altering. But God reminded them of His promise and blessing when they conceived and bore Seth. And Seth's line was significant in the whole of human history; just read the genealogy of Joseph (Jesus' earthly father) in Luke 3. Through Seth's line, God restored Adam and Eve's family back to Himself and people again worshiped Him. Finally, there was a breath of fresh air after a very sad, broken narrative.

What are the restoring lessons of Cain's story for us?

For my extended family, redemption has been slowly gained. Each child has struggled with the way their mother failed to protect them from their father—and justifiably so. But their father has passed away, and many of them have been tasked with caring for their mother, who continues to grow increasingly ill in her old age. In order to care for her, they've had to put to rest much of their residual anger and work to restore life-giving grace to their mother, herself a victim. Their restoration hasn't been perfect, but it has been beautiful to watch the healing that occurs when the mother tells her adult children that she loves them and they, in turn, forgive her.*

God took the same restorative step in His relationship with all of His children when He sent His Son to die in our place. Our relationship with Him mattered so much that He paid the greatest debt possible to reunite us with Him and guarantee it would last forever. No one says it better than the apostle Paul:

> "For God was pleased to have all His fullness dwell in Him [Jesus], and through Him to reconcile everything to Himself by making peace through the blood of His cross—whether things on earth or things in heaven. Once you were alienated and hostile in your minds because of your evil actions. But now He has reconciled you by His physical body through His death, to present you holy, faultless, and blameless before Him" (Colossians 1:19-22).

As Christians, we're called to love and forgive others, and we're never more like Christ than when we forgive. "Forgiveness is difficult," writes Archbishop Desmond Tutu, "but because we are not infallible, because we will hurt especially the ones we love by some wrong, we will always need a process

Put Yourself in Their Shoes

When a relationship goes south, the other person isn't always the one at fault. Sometimes we negatively contribute to the situation. So how do we own our part?

+ Put yourself in the other person's shoes.
+ Imagine what they think and feel.
+ Take responsibility for hurt you've caused.
+ Extend grace and forgiveness—humbly.

---

*Facilitator: Take a few minutes to tell a story of reconciliation from your life. Encourage your group members to share their own story if they have one. Hearing real stories of reconciliation is the best testimony for its power in our lives.

of forgiveness and reconciliation to deal with those unfortunate yet all too human breaches in relationships. They are an inescapable characteristic of the human condition."[7]

RECONCILIATION

Bringing together of two parties that are estranged or in dispute. Reconciliation basically means "change" or "exchange." The idea is of a change of relationship, an exchange of antagonism for good will, enmity for friendship. Attitudes are transformed and hostility ceases.

The call to forgiveness and reconciliation permeates Scripture, from Old Testament stories like Joseph and his brothers, or Hosea and Gomer, to challenges from Jesus and Paul. To let these truths sink in, read the following Scripture passages aloud:

"So if you are offering your gift on the altar, and there you remember that your brother has something against you, leave your gift there in front of the altar. First go and be reconciled with your brother, and then come and offer your gift" (Matthew 5:23-24).

"The next day he showed up while they were fighting and tried to reconcile them peacefully, saying, 'Men, you are brothers. Why are you mistreating each other?'" (Acts 7:26).

"Everything is from God, who reconciled us to Himself through Christ and gave us the ministry of reconciliation: That is, in Christ, God was reconciling the world to Himself, not counting their trespasses against them, and He has committed the message of reconciliation to us" (2 Corinthians 5:18-19).

"Therefore, God's chosen ones, holy and loved, put on heart-felt compassion, kindness, humility, gentleness, and patience, accepting one another and forgiving one another if anyone has a complaint against another. Just as the Lord has forgiven you, so you must also forgive" (Colossians 3:13).

Whether you're currently in a relationship that needs healing or are bracing for the inevitable time this will happen, it helps to fully understand the meaning and benefits of forgiveness.

Forgiveness is:

1. **Moral**—a response to an injustice; turning to the good in the face of wrongdoing
2. **Goodwill**—refusing to pursue resentment or revenge
3. **Paradoxical**—foregoing resentment or revenge when the wrongdoer's actions deserve it and giving mercy, generosity, and love when the wrongdoer doesn't deserve it
4. **Beyond duty**—a free gift (not an obligation)

Forgiveness is not:

1. **Forgetting/denying**—letting time pass or ignoring the effects of the wrongdoing
2. **Condoning**—acting as if nothing bad happened or as if it won't happen again
3. **Excusing**—like it wasn't really their responsibility
4. **Condemning**—as if she or he deserves to know they wronged you; forgiving with a sense of moral superiority
5. **Seeking justice or compensation**—forgiveness doesn't demand compensation first[8]

Restoration isn't an effortless process or a quick and easy fix. It requires time, patience, persistence, and much, much prayer. Sometimes restoration comes in the form of a dramatic event. But most often, it takes place on a small scale. It's a daily decision we make to forgive others when they sin against us, and to seek forgiveness when we do the same. In doing so, we keep bitterness from running the show. It's a way to cope with disappointment by letting go of hurt feelings. It's also a way to show them—and the world—what grace really looks like.

> GROWING WITH GOD

Spend time this week reviewing what you read in this session and what was discussed in your group time. In addition, read and pray through Hebrews 12:1-4:

> "Therefore since we also have such a large cloud of witnesses surrounding us, let us lay aside every weight and the sin that so easily ensnares us, and run with endurance the race that lies before us, keeping our eyes on Jesus, the source and perfecter of our faith, who for the joy that lay before Him endured a cross and despised the shame, and has sat down at the right hand of God's throne. For consider Him who endured such hostility from sinners against Himself, so that you won't grow weary and lose heart. In struggling against sin, you have not yet resisted to the point of shedding your blood."

This week, take the time to pray through each verse of this passage in response to sin and the encouragement the Hebrews writer gives.

Verse 1:
God, I know that sin entangles me. I also know that a sinful life isn't the way You designed Your world. Help me recognize sin when I see it and experience it, and give me the courage and strength to literally strip it off and to stand up to it. You've called me to much more than what sin would allow—help me run toward that life, which is in Christ.

Verse 2:
Jesus, You have the power to perfect my faith. May it be perfected as I trust You to guide me around the minefield of sin.

Verse 3:
Jesus, You understand sin better than I ever could. Your whole life on earth was riddled with the attack of sin. Yet You persevered and showed me what it means to live sinlessly and to respond in a godly way to sin when it attacks. I may not be You, but You've given me the power of the Holy Spirit to endure.

_____

Verse 4:

Jesus, You lost Your life because of sin's effect on mankind. May I not lose my life, but rather find it in You. My struggle with sin must pale in comparison to the joy I find in knowing You. As I know You more, will You teach me more about how to resist sin? In doing so, I give You all praise.

> MAKING A CHANGE

1. On an index card, write the name of one person you've sinned against and disrupted the relationship. On the back of the card, write down three ways you can reach out to that person, and put an asterisk next to the one thing you intend to do this week. Carry this card in your purse or pocket, and pray over that relationship and your reconciliation as you prepare to reach out.

2. A broken relationship is a lot more difficult to mend when you weren't the one who broke it. Who among your Christian brothers and sisters has most deeply injured your soul?
   - Write their names down in the space below.
   - Next to each name, write your answer to the questions, *What does love want of me in this situation? What would love have me do in response to this person?*
   - Then, some time in the next four weeks, do it.

_____

_____

_____

_____

_____

LETTING GO

Sometimes the best thing you can do for a friendship is learn to let go. But how do you know when it's time to stop the pursuit of a relationship that's stagnated or fallen apart? If you're making all the effort—always the one calling or suggesting times to get together—it may be time to think about investing your energy in other relationships. If a friend hasn't been responsive to your efforts, recognize that the timing may not be right to revitalize a relationship. You can continue to care for your friend and at the same time let the active involvement in each other's lives go. A friendship reconnection can always be revisited later when the time is right for both of you.

END NOTES

SESSION 1

1. Dietrich Bonhoeffer, *Life Together: The Classic Exploration of Christian Community* (New York: Harper & Row Publishers, Inc., 1954), 25.

2. Andy Stanley, *Five Things God Uses to Grow Your Faith Participant's Guide* (Grand Rapids, Michigan: Zondervan, 2009), 31.

3. Beth Moore, *Stepping Up: A Journey Through the Psalms of Ascent* (Nashville: LifeWay Press, 2008), 161.

4. Moore, *Stepping Up: A Journey Through the Psalms of Ascent,* 156.

SESSION 2

1. "Aristotle Quotes," 2011 [cited 30 August 2011]. Available from the Internet: *www.brainyquotes.net.*

2. Oswald Chambers, *My Utmost for His Highest* (New York: Dodd, Mead & Company, 1935), 7.

3. John Piper, *What Jesus Demands from the World* (Wheaton, Illinois: Crossway Books, 2006), 253.

4. Dorothy C. Bass and Susan R. Briehl, eds., *On Our Way: Christian Practices for Living a Whole Life* (Nashville: Upper Room Books, 2010), 74, 77.

SESSION 3

1. "Henri Nouwen Quotes," 2011 [cited 30 August 2011]. Available from the Internet: *www.brainyquotes.net.*

2. "Andrew Carnegie Quotes," 2011 [cited 30 August 2011]. Available from the Internet: *www.quotestar.com.*

3. Margaret Feinberg, *Scouting the Divine: Searching for God in Wine, Wool, and Wild Honey* (Nashville: LifeWay Press, 2010), 115.

4. David G. Benner, *Sacred Companions: The Gift of Spiritual Friendship & Direction* (Downers Grove, Illinois: InterVarsity Press, 2002), 73-74.

5. Compiled by Lucinda Vardy, *Mother Teresa: A Simple Path* (New York: Ballantine Books, 1995), 80.

SESSION 4

1. "Victor Hugo Quotes," 2011 [cited 30 August 2011]. Available from the Internet: *www.brainyquotes.net*.

2. Ken Sande and Kevin Johnson, *The Peacemaker Student Edition: Handling Conflict without Fighting Back or Running Away* (Grand Rapids, Michigan: Baker Books, 2008), 7.

3. Adapted from Sande and Johnson, *The Peacemaker Student Edition*, 16, and from the Internet: *www.all-things-conflict-resolution-and-adr.com/Workplace-Conflict-Resolution.html*.

4. From John Walton, *The NIV Application Commentary: Genesis* (Grand Rapids, Michigan: Zondervan, 2001), 270.

5. Matt Carter and Halim Suh, *Creation Unraveled: The Gospel According to Genesis* (Nashville: LifeWay Press, 2011), 70.

6. Joshua Horwitz and Naomi Rosenblatt, *Wrestling With Angels* (New York: Delta Books, 1995), 57.

7. Desmond Tutu, *No Future Without Forgiveness* (New York: Doubleday, 2000).

8. Adapted from The International Forgiveness Institute. Available from the Internet: *www.forgiveness-institute.org*.

Threads

An advocate of churches and people like you, Threads provides Bible studies and events designed to:

CULTIVATE COMMUNITY We need people we can call when the tire's flat or when we get the promotion. And it's those people—the day-in-day-out people—who we want to walk through life with and learn about God from.

PROVIDE DEPTH Kiddie pools are for kids. We're looking to dive in, head first, to all the hard-to-talk-about topics, tough questions, and thought-provoking Scriptures. We think this is a good thing, because we're in process. We're becoming. And who we're becoming isn't shallow.

LIFT UP RESPONSIBILITY We are committed to being responsible—doing the right things like recycling and volunteering. And we're also trying to grow in our understanding of what it means to share the gospel, serve the poor, love our neighbors, tithe, and make wise choices about our time, money, and relationships.

ENCOURAGE CONNECTION We're looking for connection with our church, our community, with somebody who's willing to walk along side us and give us a little advice here and there. We'd like opportunities to pour our lives out for others because we're willing to do that walk-along-side thing for someone else, too. We have a lot to learn from people older and younger than us. From the body of Christ.

We're glad you picked up this study. Please come by and visit us at *threadsmedia.com*.

ALSO FROM THREADS . . .

CREATION UNRAVELED
THE GOSPEL ACCORDING TO GENESIS
BY MATT CARTER & HALIM SUH

More than a collection of stories, the Bible tells one story—God's story of bringing us back to Himself after sin infiltrated a good world and caused the unraveling of creation. Join authors Matt Carter and Halim Suh as they examine Genesis 1–11 and explore how the first chapters of the Bible lay the foundation for the gospel of Jesus Christ—the good news of salvation and redemption that we find only in relationship with Him.

Matt Carter serves as lead pastor of The Austin Stone Community Church in Austin, Texas. He is also a cancer survivor, author, and speaker for camps and conferences nationwide. Halim Suh is an elder and pastor of equipping at The Austin Stone Community Church.

MENTOR
HOW ALONG-THE-WAY DISCIPLESHIP WILL CHANGE YOUR LIFE
BY CHUCK LAWLESS

Drawing from biblical examples like Jesus and His disciples and Paul and Timothy, author Chuck Lawless explores the life-transforming process of a mentoring relationship. This study is both a practical and spiritual guide to biblical mentoring, providing easy-to-model life application for how to have and be a mentor.

Chuck Lawless is vice president for Global Theological Advance of the International Mission Board. The author of several books, Dr. Lawless is also president of the Lawless Group, a church consulting firm (thelawlessgroup.com).

INTERRUPTED
AN ADVENTURE IN RELEARNING THE ESSENTIALS OF FAITH
BY JEN HATMAKER

Believe it or not, the American Dream and Christianity aren't the same thing, and God is in the business of interrupting what we think our lives are about. Author Jen Hatmaker argues that we've missed the point, confusing Christianity with the American Dream and manipulating Scripture to say what we want it to say. Interrupted is about freedom from consumer-driven Christianity and getting back to true faith, real life, real justice, real religion.

Jen Hatmaker lives in Austin, Texas, where in 2008 she and her husband Brandon started Austin New Church, a community of faith obsessed about bringing justice and restoration to the city and the world. Jen has written several books and Bible studies. She travels all over the United States speaking at conferences and retreats.

readsmedia.com
800.458.2772
feWay Christian Stores

FOR FULL DETAILS ON ALL OF THREADS' STUDIES, VISIT *THREADSMEDIA.COM*.

GROUP CONTACT INFORMATION

Name _____ Number _____
E-mail _____

Name _____ Number _____
E-mail _____

Name _____ Number _____
E-mail _____

Name _____ Number _____
E-mail _____

Name _____ Number _____
E-mail _____

Name _____ Number _____
E-mail _____

Name _____ Number _____
E-mail _____

Name _____ Number _____
E-mail _____

Name _____ Number _____
E-mail _____